CW00495570

Half Baked Harvest Recipes

Quick and tasty recipes for the whole family. Recipes for instant, nightly, meal-ready and easy-to-prepare foods a cookbook

TABLE OF CONTENTS

BREAKFAST 8

Egg baked in avocado 8
Cheese Crepes 10
Ricotta Pancakes 12
Yogurt Waffles 14
Broccoli Muffins 17
Pumpkin Bread 19
Eggs in Avocado Cups 21
Cheddar Scramble 22
Bacon Omelet 23

APPETIZER AND SIDES 25

Potato and Spinach Mix 25
Balsamic Squash Mix 27
Turmeric Potatoes 28
Bacon Potato Mix 30
Coconut Sprouts Salad 31

LUNCH 33

Lime Chicken with Savoy Cabbage 34
Middle Eastern Lamb Zucchini Casserole 36
Ginger Steak Broccoli 39
BLT Chicken Salad 41

DINNER 43

Chili Zucchini Beef Lasagna 43
Rib Roast with Roasted Red Shallots and Garlic 45
Beef Ragù With A Twist 47
Lemon Pork Chops with Buttered Brussels Sprouts 50
Ground Pork & Scrambled Eggs with Cabbage 52
Cheeseburger Skillet with Bacon & Mushrooms 54
Traditional Beef Bourguignon 57

Basil Prosciutto Pizza 58
Keto Crispy Rosemary Chicken Drumsticks 60
Baked Pesto Chicken 61

SOUP AND STEWS 62

Best Broccoli Cheddar Soup 62
Best Cream of Broccoli Soup 64
Curried Butternut Squash Soup 66
Roasted Tomato Basil Soup 68
Creamy Sweet Potato Soup 70
Hearty Beef and Vegetable Stew 71

VEGETABLES 73

Innovated Shrimp Salad 73
Citrusy Scallops with Pomegranate 75
Brisk Mediterranean Chicken Salad 77
Spicy Tamarind Tinged Shrimp Salad 80
Natural Lobster Salad 83

SNACK AND DESSERTS 85

Chocolate Cupcakes 85
Chocolate Chip Mug Cake 87
Creamy Coconut Hazelnut Cake 89
Ice Cream Brownies 92
Mint Brownies with Hazelnuts 94
Mocha Pots de Creme 96
Chocolate Chip Pudding 98
Vanilla Cherry Panna Cotta 100
Orange Lime Pudding 102
Guacamole Deviled Eggs 104
Double Chocolate Chip Cookies 107

© Copyright 2020 by Nicol Rodari - All rights reserved.

The following Book is reproduced below with the goal of providing information that is as accurate and reliable as possible. Regardless, purchasing this Book can be seen as consent to the fact that both the publisher and the author of this book are in no way experts on the topics discussed within and that any recommendations or suggestions that are made herein are for entertainment purposes only. Professionals should be consulted as needed prior to undertaking any of the action endorsed herein.

This declaration is deemed fair and valid by both the American Bar Association and the Committee of Publishers Association and is legally binding throughout the United States.

Furthermore, the transmission, duplication, or reproduction of any of the following work including specific information will be considered an illegal act irrespective of if it is done electronically or in print. This extends to creating a secondary or tertiary copy of the work or a recorded copy and is only allowed with the express written consent from the Publisher. All additional right reserved.

The information in the following pages is broadly considered a truthful and accurate account of facts and as such, any inattention, use, or misuse of the information in question by the reader will render any resulting actions solely under their purview. There are no scenarios in which the publisher or the original author of this work can be in any fashion deemed liable for any hardship or damages that may befall them after undertaking information described herein.

Additionally, the information in the following pages is intended only for informational purposes and should thus be thought of as universal. As befitting its nature, it is presented without assurance regarding its prolonged validity or interim quality. Trademarks that are mentioned are done without written consent and can in no way be considered an endorsement from the trademark holder.

BREAKFAST

Egg baked in avocado

Preparation Time: 5 Minutes

Cooking Time: 15 Minutes

Servings: 2

Ingredients:

- One large ripe avocado
- Two large eggs
- Salt
- Freshly ground black pepper
- Four tablespoons jarred pesto, for serving
- Two tablespoons chopped tomato, for serving
- Two tablespoons crumbled feta, for serving (optional)

Directions:

1. Preheat the oven to 425 F.
2. Cut the avocado in and take away the pit. Scoop out about 1 to 2 tablespoons from each half to create a hole large enough to fit an egg. Place the avocado halves on a baking sheet, cut-side up.
3. Crack one egg in each avocado half and season with pepper and salt.
4. Bake and wait for the eggs are set and cooked to the wanted level of doneness, 10 to 15 minutes.
5. Remove from oven and top each avocado with two tablespoons pesto, one tablespoon chopped tomato, and one tablespoon crumbled feta (if using).

Nutrition: Calories: 302 Total Fat,: 26g Total Carbs: 10g Protein: 8g

Cheese Crepes

Preparation Time: 15 Minutes

Cooking Time: 20 Minutes

Servings: 5

Ingredients:

- 6 ounces cream cheese
- 1/3 cup Parmesan cheese
- Six large organic eggs
- One teaspoon granulated erythritol
- 1½ tablespoon coconut flour
- 1/8 teaspoon xanthan gum
- Two tablespoons unsalted butter

Directions:

1. Pulse the cream cheese, Parmesan cheese, eggs, and erythritol using a blender.
2. Place the coconut flour and xanthan gum and pulse again.
3. Now, pulse at medium speed. Transfer and put aside within 5 minutes.
4. Melt butter over medium-low heat.
5. Place one portion of the mixture and tilt the pan to spread into a thin layer.
6. Cook within 1½ minutes.
7. Flip the crepe and cook within 15-20 seconds more. Serve.

Nutrition: Calories 297 Net Carbs 1.9 g Total Fat 25.1 g Cholesterol 281 mg Total Carbs 3.5 g Protein 13.7 g

Ricotta Pancakes

Preparation Time: 10 Minutes

Cooking Time: 20 Minutes

Servings: 4

Ingredients:

- Four organic eggs
- ½ cup ricotta cheese
- ¼ cup of vanilla whey protein powder
- ½ teaspoon organic baking powder
- Salt
- ½ teaspoon liquid stevia
- Two tablespoons unsalted butter

Directions:

1. Pulse all the fixing in the blender.
2. Warm-up butter over medium heat.
3. Put the batter and spread it evenly—Cook within 2 minutes.
4. Flip and cook again within 1–2 minutes. Serve.

Nutrition: Calories 184 Net Carbs 2.7 g Total Fat 12.9 g Total Carbs 2.7 g Protein 14.6 g

Yogurt Waffles

Preparation Time: 15 Minutes

Cooking Time: 25 Minutes

Servings: 5

Ingredients:

- ½ cup golden flax seeds meal
- ½ cup plus three tablespoons almond flour
- 1-1½ tablespoons granulated erythritol
- One tablespoon of vanilla whey protein powder
- ¼ teaspoon baking soda
- ½ teaspoon organic baking powder
- ¼ teaspoon xanthan gum
- Salt
- One large organic egg
- One organic egg
- Two tablespoons unsweetened almond milk
- 1½ tablespoons unsalted butter
- 3 ounces plain Greek yogurt

Directions:

1. Preheat the waffle iron, then grease it.
2. Mix add the flour, erythritol, protein powder, baking soda, baking powder, xanthan gum, and salt.
3. Beat the egg white until stiff peaks. In a third bowl, add two egg yolks, whole egg, almond milk, butter, yogurt, and beat.

4. Put egg mixture into the bowl of the flour mixture and mix.
5. Gently fold in the beaten egg whites. Place ¼ cup of the mixture into preheated waffle iron and cook for about 4–5 minutes. Serve.

Nutrition: Calories 250 Net Carbs 3.2 g Total Fat 18.7 g Protein 8.4 g

Broccoli Muffins

Preparation Time: 15 Minutes

Cooking Time: 20 Minutes

Servings: 6

Ingredients:

- Two tablespoons unsalted butter
- Six large organic eggs
- ½ cup heavy whipping cream
- ½ cup Parmesan cheese
- Salt & ground black pepper
- 1¼ cups broccoli
- Two tablespoons parsley
- ½ cup Swiss cheese

Directions:

1. Warm-up oven to 350°F, then grease a 12-cup muffin tin.
2. Mix the eggs, cream, Parmesan cheese, salt, and black pepper.
3. Divide the broccoli and parsley in the muffin cup.
4. Top with the egg mixture, with Swiss cheese.
5. Bake within 20 minutes. Cool for about 5 minutes. Serve.

Nutrition: Calories 231 Net Carbs 2 g Total Fat 18.1 g Cholesterol 228 mg Protein 13.5 g

Pumpkin Bread

Preparation Time: 15 Minutes

Cooking Time: 60 Minutes

Servings: 16

Ingredients:

- 1 2/3 cups almond flour
- 1½ teaspoons organic baking powder
- ½ teaspoon pumpkin pie spice
- ½ teaspoon cinnamon
- ½ teaspoon cloves
- ½ teaspoon salt
- 8 ounces cream cheese
- Six organic eggs
- One tablespoon coconut flour
- 1 cup powdered erythritol
- One teaspoon stevia powder
- One teaspoon organic lemon extract
- 1 cup pumpkin puree
- ½ cup of coconut oil

Directions:

1. Warm-up oven to 325°F. Grease 2 bread loaf pans.
2. Mix the almond flour, baking powder, spices, and salt in a small bowl.

3. In a second bowl, add the cream cheese, one egg, coconut flour, ¼ cup of erythritol, and ¼ teaspoon of the stevia, and beat.
4. In a third bowl, add the pumpkin puree, oil, five eggs, ¾ cup of the erythritol, and ¾ teaspoon of the stevia and mix.
5. Mix the pumpkin mixture into the bowl of the flour mixture.
6. Place about ¼ of the pumpkin mixture into each loaf pan.
7. Top each pan with the cream cheese mixture, plus the rest pumpkin mixture.
8. Bake within 50–60 minutes. Cold within 10 minutes. Slice and serve.

Nutrition: Calories 216 Net Carbs 2.5 g Total Fat 19.8 g Cholesterol 77 mg Protein 3.4 g

Eggs in Avocado Cups

Preparation Time: 10 Minutes

Cooking Time: 20 Minutes

Servings: 4

Ingredients:

- Two avocados
- Four organic eggs
- Salt
- Ground black pepper
- Four tablespoons cheddar cheese
- Two cooked bacon
- One tablespoon scallion green

Directions:

1. Warm-up oven to 400°F. Remove two tablespoons of flesh from the avocado.
2. Place avocado halves into a small baking dish.
3. Crack an egg in each avocado half and sprinkle with salt plus black pepper.
4. Top each egg with cheddar cheese evenly.
5. Bake within 20 minutes. Serve with bacon and chives.

Nutrition: Calories 343 Net Carbs 2.2 g Total Fat 29.1 g Cholesterol 186 mg Protein 13.8 g

Cheddar Scramble

Preparation Time: 10 Minutes

Cooking Time: 8 Minutes

Servings: 6

Ingredients:

- Two tablespoons olive oil
- One small yellow onion
- 12 large organic eggs
- Salt and ground black pepper
- 4 ounces cheddar cheese

Directions:

1. Warm-up oil over medium heat.
2. Sauté the onion within 4–5 minutes.
3. Add the eggs, salt, and black pepper and cook within 3 minutes.
4. Remove then stir in the cheese. Serve.

Nutrition: Calories 264 Net Carbs 1.8 g Total Fat 20.9 g Cholesterol 392 mg Protein 17.4 g

Bacon Omelet

Preparation Time: 10 Minutes

Cooking Time: 15 Minutes

Servings: 2

Ingredients:

- Four organic eggs
- One tablespoon chive
- Salt
- ground black pepper
- Four bacon slices
- One tablespoon unsalted butter
- 2 ounces cheddar cheese

Directions:

1. Beat the eggs, chives, salt, and black pepper in a bowl.
2. Warm-up a pan over medium-high heat then cooks the bacon slices within 8–10 minutes.
3. Chop the bacon slices. Melt butter and cook the egg mixture within 2 minutes.
4. Flip the omelet and top with chopped bacon. Cook within 1–2 minutes.
5. Remove then put the cheese in the center of the omelet. Serve.

Nutrition: Calories 427 Net Carbs 1.2 g Total Fat 28.2 g Cholesterol 469 mg Protein 29.1 g

APPETIZER AND SIDES

Potato and Spinach Mix

Preparation Time: 10 minutes

Cooking Time: 30 minutes

Servings: 4

Ingredients:

- 3 sweet potatoes, cut into medium chunks
- 1 tablespoon olive oil
- 4 ounces baby spinach, torn
- A pinch of salt and black pepper
- ½ cup onion, chopped
- 2 tablespoons balsamic vinegar
- 2 tablespoons lemon juice
- 1 avocado, peeled, pitted, and chopped

Directions:

1. Arrange the potato pieces on a lined baking sheet, add oil, salt and pepper, toss and bake for 30 minutes at 400 degrees F. Transfer to a bowl, add the rest of the ingredients, toss and serve.

Nutrition: 185 Calories 6g Fat 6g Fiber 10g Carbs 3g Protein

Balsamic Squash Mix

Preparation Time: 10 minutes

Cooking Time: 45 minutes

Servings: 4

Ingredients:

- 1 acorn squash, seeded and sliced into medium pieces
- Salt, to taste
- 4 cups kale, chopped
- 1 tablespoon olive oil
- 3 tablespoons pomegranate seeds
- ¼ cup walnuts, toasted
- For the salad dressing:
- 1½ teaspoons balsamic vinegar
- 1 teaspoon olive oil
- ½ teaspoon mustard
- A pinch of salt

Directions:

1. Arrange the squash on a lined baking sheet, add oil and salt, toss, bake in the oven at 400ºF for 40 minutes, and transfer to a bowl. In a salad bowl, mix the squash with the kale and the rest of the ingredients, toss and serve as a side dish.

Nutrition: 300 Calories 12g Fat 11g Fiber 30g Carbs 8g Protein

Turmeric Potatoes

Preparation Time: 10 minutes

Cooking Time: 30 minutes

Servings: 4

Ingredients:

- 8 sweet potatoes
- 1 teaspoon turmeric powder
- 3 tablespoons olive oil
- ½ teaspoon ground ginger
- Salt and ground black pepper, to taste
- 1 bunch fresh parsley
- Juice of 1 lemon
- 1 garlic clove

Directions:

1. In a baking dish, mix the sweet potatoes with the turmeric and the other ingredients, toss and bake in the oven at 400ºF for 30 minutes. Divide between plates and serve as a side dish.

Nutrition: 230 Calories 3g Fat 6g Fiber 9g Carbs 10g Protein

Bacon Potato Mix

Preparation Time: 10 minutes

Cooking Time: 30 minutes

Servings: 4

Ingredients:

- 7 bacon slices
- 1½ pounds potatoes, cut into rounds
- 2 garlic cloves
- 1 tablespoon sage, chopped
- 1 tablespoon fresh rosemary
- Salt and ground black pepper to taste

Directions:

1. Put the potatoes in a pot, add water to cover, also add some salt, bring to a boil over medium-high heat, cook for 6 minutes and drain. Heat a pan over medium-high heat, add the bacon, stir, brown for 10 minutes, and transfer to a bowl. Add the potatoes and the rest of the ingredients to the pan, and cook for 20 minutes, stirring often. Add the bacon, toss, divide between plates and serve.

Nutrition: 300 Calories 12g Fat 4g Fiber 20g Carbs 4g Protein

Coconut Sprouts Salad

Preparation Time: 10 minutes

Cooking Time: 30 minutes

Servings: 8

Ingredients:

- 2¼ pounds Brussels sprouts, halved
- Salt and ground black pepper, to taste
- 3 tablespoons coconut oil, melted
- For the dressing:
- 1 tablespoon fresh ginger, grated
- 1 tablespoon olive oil
- 1 shallot, peeled and chopped
- 2 garlic cloves, peeled and minced
- 3 tablespoons coconut amino
- ⅓ cup orange juice
- 1½ tablespoons balsamic vinegar
- ¼ cup fresh cilantro, chopped
- 1½ tablespoons sesame seeds, toasted

Directions:

1. In a roasting pan, mix the sprouts with the coconut oil, salt and pepper, toss, and bake in the oven at 375ºF for 20 minutes. Meanwhile, heat a pan with the olive oil over medium high heat, add the shallot and the ginger, stir and cook for 2 minutes.

2. Add the garlic, stir and cook for 1 minute more. Add the amino, the baked sprouts and the rest of the ingredients, toss, cook for 5-6 more minutes, divide between plates and serve.

Nutrition: 200 Calories 4g Fat 4g Fiber 7g Carbs 6g Protein

LUNCH

Lime Chicken with Savoy Cabbage

Preparation Time: 10 Minutes

Cooking Time: 7 Hours

Servings: 4

Ingredients:

- Eight chicken thighs, skinless
- 2 cups Savoy cabbage, chopped
- One stalk celery, diced
- One medium onion, diced
- 1 tbsp ginger, grated
- ½ cup chicken stock
- Two limes
- 1 tsp salt
- 1 tsp black pepper
- Extra virgin olive oil
- Spicy squash noodles for serving

Directions:

1. Place 4 tbsp extra virgin olive oil in a slow cooker, spread around the bottom. Add the ginger and onions.

2. Slice lime into ½" thick circles. Place chicken in the bottom of a slow cooker, and sprinkle with ½ tsp salt and ½ tsp black pepper. Top with lime slices.
3. On top of those, place the celery and cabbage.
4. Pour in chicken stock, then cook on Low for 7 hours.
5. Serve with Spicy Squash Noodles.

Nutrition: Calories 273 Carbs 5.7 g Fat 12 g Protein 34 g

Middle Eastern Lamb Zucchini Casserole

Preparation Time: 20 Minutes

Cooking Time: 7 Hours

Servings: 6

Ingredients:

- Four zucchinis, peeled
- 1 lb. ground lamb
- ½ cup coconut cream
- Two eggs
- ¼ cup Parmesan
- ½ tsp cinnamon
- ½ tsp cloves
- ½ tsp cumin
- 1 tsp salt
- 1 tsp black pepper
- Extra virgin olive oil

Directions:

1. Use a mandolin, thinly-slice zucchini lengthwise.
2. Heat 3 tbsp extra virgin olive oil in the skillet. Add lamb, cinnamon, cloves, and cumin. Brown.
3. Combine coconut cream with egg, salt, and black pepper—coat slow cooker with olive oil, place ¼ of zucchini strips on the slow cooker's bottom.

4. Next, brush coconut cream mixture on zucchini.
5. Place another layer of zucchini and half the remaining coconut cream, top with lamb, another layer of zucchini, remaining coconut cream.
6. Cook on Low for 7 hours.

Nutrition: Calories 203 Carbs 4.7 g Fat 10 g Protein 25 g

Ginger Steak Broccoli

Preparation Time: 10 Minutes

Cooking Time: 4 Hours

Servings: 4

Ingredients:

- 1 lb. sirloin steak
- 3 cups broccoli florets (frozen okay)
- 1 cup low-sodium beef stock
- 1 tbsp grated ginger
- ½ tsp thyme
- 1 tsp salt
- 1 tsp black pepper
- Extra virgin olive oil

Directions:

- Slice sirloin steak against the grain into ½" wide strips.
- Place 4 tbsp extra virgin olive oil in a skillet, add steak, and brown for a minute on each side.
- Place steak, broccoli florets, along with ginger, beef stock, and soy sauce in a slow cooker.
- Cook on medium-high for 4 hours.
- Enjoy alone or with cauliflower rice.

Nutrition: Calories 273 Carbs 6 g Fat 11 g Protein 37 g Sodium 714 mg

BLT Chicken Salad

Preparation Time: 20 Minutes

Cooking Time: 4 Hours

Servings: 4

Ingredients:

- 4 x 4oz chicken breast
- 2 cup low-sodium chicken broth
- Eight slices bacon
- 2 cups romaine lettuce
- One tomato, diced
- 1 tsp salt
- 1 tsp black pepper
- ¼ cup organic mayonnaise
- Extra virgin olive oil

Directions:

1. Coat slow cooker with a little olive oil, and set on high.
2. Tenderize chicken breast, and sprinkle each chicken breast with salt and black pepper.
3. Wrap each chicken breast with bacon, and place it in a slow cooker.
4. Cook chicken breast on high for 4 hours.
5. Place mayonnaise with 1 tsp black pepper and 4 tbsp extra virgin olive oil in a blender. Mix until smooth.

6. Combine lettuce, tomato in a bowl, and toss with mayo dressing.
7. Top salad with chicken breast and serve.

Nutrition: Calories 366 Carbs 6 g Fat 19 g Protein 43 g Sodium 1183 mg

DINNER

Chili Zucchini Beef Lasagna

Preparation Time: 5 Minutes

Cooking Time: 55 Minutes

Servings: 4

Ingredients:

- ½ cup Pecorino Romano cheese
- Four yellow zucchinis, sliced
- Salt and black pepper to taste
- 1 tbsp lard
- ½ lb. ground beef
- 1 tsp garlic powder
- 1 tsp onion powder
- 2 tbsp coconut flour
- 1 ½ cups grated mozzarella
- 2 cups crumbled goat cheese
- 1 large egg
- 2 cups marinara sauce
- 1 tbsp Italian herb seasoning
- ¼ tsp red chili flakes
- ¼ cup fresh basil leaves

Directions:

1. Preheat oven to 375 F
2. Melt the lard in a skillet t and cook beef for minutes; set aside.
3. In a bowl, combine garlic powder, onion powder, coconut flour, salt, pepper, mozzarella cheese, half of Pecorino cheese, goat cheese, and egg.
4. Mix Italian herb seasoning and chili flakes with marinara sauce.
5. Make a single layer of the zucchini in a greased baking dish, spread ¼ of the egg mixture on top, and ¼ of the marinara sauce.
6. Repeat the process. Top it with the remaining Pecorino cheese.
7. Bake in the oven for 20 minutes. Garnish with basil, slice, and serve.

Nutrition: Cal 608 Net Carbs 5.5g Fat 37g Protein 52g

Rib Roast with Roasted Red Shallots and Garlic

Preparation Time: 5 Minutes

Cooking Time: 55 Minutes

Servings: 6

Ingredients:

- 5 lb. beef rib roast, on the bone
- Three heads garlic, cut in half
- 3 tbsp olive oil
- Six shallots, peeled and halved
- Two lemons, zested and juiced
- 3 tbsp mustard seeds
- 3 tbsp swerve
- Salt and black pepper to taste
- 3 tbsp thyme leaves

Directions:

1. Preheat oven to 450ºF. Place garlic heads and shallots in a roasting dish, toss with olive oil, and bake for minutes.
2. Pour lemon juice on them. Score shallow crisscrosses patterns on the meat and set aside.
3. Mix swerve, mustard seeds, thyme, salt, pepper, and lemon zest to make a rub; and apply it all over the beef.

4. Place the beef on the shallots and garlic; cook in the oven for 15 minutes. Reduce the heat to 400ºF, cover the dish with foil, and continue cooking for 5 minutes.
5. Once ready, remove the dish, and let sit covered for 15 minutes before slicing.

Nutrition: Cal 556 Fat 38.6g Net Carbs 2.5g Protein 58.4g

Beef Ragù With A Twist

Preparation Time: 5 Minutes

Cooking Time: 25 Minutes

Servings: 6

Ingredients:

- 1 ½ pounds ground beef
- One bell pepper, deseeded and chopped
- 1 celery rib, chopped
- 1/2 cup shallots, chopped
- Two garlic cloves, chopped
- Two vine-ripe tomatoes, pureed
- 2 cups beef bone broth
- One tablespoon dried Italian herb seasoning

Directions:

1. In a lightly greased stockpot, brown the ground beef until no longer pink or about 5 minutes, crumbling with a spatula; reserve.
2. In the same pot, sauté the peppers, celery, and shallots, adding broth as needed. Continue to sauté until they have softened.
3. Now, stir in the garlic and continue to sauté for 40 seconds more. Add in the pureed tomatoes, beef bone broth, and Italian herb seasoning, bringing to a boil. Return the reserved beef to the pot.

4. Reduce heat to medium-low. Continue to simmer until the sauce has reduced to half of the volume or about 15 minutes. Bon appétit!

Nutrition: Calories 349 Fat 21.8g Carbs 4.9g Protein 34g Fiber 1.4g

Lemon Pork Chops with Buttered Brussels Sprouts

Preparation Time: 5 Minutes

Cooking Time: 27 Minutes

Servings: 6

Ingredients:

- 3 tbsp lemon juice
- Three cloves garlic, pureed
- 1 tbsp olive oil
- Six pork loin chops
- 1 tbsp butter
- 1 lb. brussels sprouts, trimmed and halved
- 2 tbsp white wine
- Salt and black pepper to taste

Directions:

1. Preheat broiler to 400ºF and mix the lemon juice, garlic, salt, black pepper, and oil in a bowl.
2. Brush the pork with the mixture, place on a baking sheet, and cook for 6 minutes on each side until browned.
3. Share into six plates and make the side dish.
4. Melt butter in a small wok or pan and cook in brussels sprouts for 5 minutes until tender.

5. Drizzle with white wine, sprinkle with salt and black pepper, and cook for another 5 minutes.
6. Ladle brussels sprouts to the side of the chops and serve with a hot sauce.

Nutrition: Cal 54Fat 48g Net Carbs 2g Protein 26g

Ground Pork & Scrambled Eggs with Cabbage

Preparation Time: 5 Minutes

Cooking Time: 30 Minutes

Servings: 4

Ingredients:

- 2 tbsp sesame oil
- Two large eggs
- 2 tbsp minced garlic
- ½ tsp ginger puree
- One medium white onion, diced
- 1 lb. ground pork
- One habanero pepper, chopped
- One green cabbage, shredded
- Five scallions, chopped
- 3 tbsp coconut aminos
- 1 tbsp white vinegar
- 2 tbsp sesame seeds

Directions:

1. Heat tbsp of sesame oil in a skillet over and scramble the eggs until set, 1 minute; set aside.
2. Heat 1 tbsp sesame oil in the same skillet and sauté garlic, ginger, and onion until soft and fragrant, 4 minutes.

3. Add ground pork and habanero pepper and season with salt, pepper. Cook for 10 minutes.
4. Mix in cabbage, scallions, aminos, and vinegar and cook until the cabbage is tender. Stir in the eggs.
5. Serve garnished with sesame seeds and some low carb tortillas.

Nutrition: Cal 295 Net Carbs 3.6g Fat 16g Protein 29g

Cheeseburger Skillet with Bacon & Mushrooms

Preparation Time: 5 Minutes

Cooking Time: 20 Minutes

Servings: 4

Ingredients:

- Two slices Canadian bacon, chopped
- 1/2 cup shallots, sliced
- 1 garlic clove, minced
- 1-pound ground pork
- Sea salt and ground black pepper
- 1/3 cup vegetable broth
- 1/4 cup white wine
- 6 ounces Cremini mushrooms, sliced
- 1/2 cup cream cheese

Directions:

1. Heat a cast-iron skillet.
2. Cook the bacon and reserve the bacon and tablespoon of fat. Then, sauté the shallots and garlic in 1 tablespoon of bacon fat until tender and fragrant.
3. Add the ground pork, salt, and black pepper to the skillet. Cook for 4 to 5 minutes or until ground meat is nicely browned.

4. Add broth, wine, and mushrooms. Close the lid, then cook for 8 to 9 minutes over medium flame.
5. Turn off the heat. Add cream cheese and stir to combine. Serve topped with the reserved bacon. Enjoy!

Nutrition: Calories 463Fat 60g Carbs 4.7g Fiber 0.8g Protein 36.2g

Traditional Beef Bourguignon

Preparation Time: 5 Minutes

Cooking Time: 1 Hour and 20 Minutes

Servings: 5

Ingredients:

- 1 ½ pounds shoulder steak, cut into cubes
- One tablespoon Herbs de Provence
- 1 onion, chopped
- 1 celery stalk, chopped
- 1 cup red Burgundy wine

Directions:

1. Heat a lightly greased soup pot over a medium-high flame. Now brown the beef in batches until no longer pink.
2. Add a splash of wine to deglaze your pan.
3. Add the Herbs de Provence, onion, celery, and wine to the pot; pour in cups of water and stir to combine well. Bring to a rapid boil; then, turn the heat to medium-low.
4. Close the lid and simmer for 1 hour 10 minutes. Serve over hot cauliflower rice if desired. Enjoy!

Nutrition: Calories 217 Fat 5.5g Carbs 3.9g Protein 30g Fiber 0.4g

Basil Prosciutto Pizza

Preparation Time: 5 Minutes

Cooking Time: 45 Minutes

Servings: 4

Ingredients:

- Four prosciutto slices, cut into thirds
- 2 cups grated mozzarella cheese
- 2 tbsp cream cheese, softened
- ½ cup almond flour
- 1 egg, beaten
- 1/3 cup tomato sauce
- 1/3 cup sliced mozzarella
- Six fresh basil leaves, to serve

Directions:

1. Preheat oven to 390 F
2. Microwave mozzarella cheese and 2 tbsp of cream cheese for a minute.
3. Mix in almond meal and egg.
4. Spread the mixture on the pizza pan and bake for 15 minutes; set aside.
5. Spread the tomato sauce on the crust. Arrange the mozzarella slices on the sauce and then the prosciutto.
6. Bake again for 15 minutes or wait until the cheese melts.

7. Remove and top with the basil. Slice and serve.

Nutrition: Cal 160 Net Carbs 0.5g Fats 6.2g Protein 22g

Keto Crispy Rosemary Chicken Drumsticks

Preparation Time: 10 Minutes

Cooking Time: 40 Minutes

Servings: 4

Ingredients:

- 12 chicken drumsticks
- 4 tbsp. olive oil
- 4 tbsp. rosemary leaves
- 2 tsp. salt

Directions:

1. Preheat oven to 450 F.
2. Rub salt and rosemary on each chicken drumstick the blend and spot on a lubed heating plate.
3. Make sure the drumsticks are not contacting each other on the plate. Drizzle the olive oil or avocado oil over the chicken drumsticks.
4. Prepare for 40 minutes until the skin is firm.

Nutrition: Calories 473 Fat 32 g Carbs 6 g Protein 42 g

Baked Pesto Chicken

Preparation Time: 5 Minutes

Cooking Time: 35 Minutes

Servings: 4

Ingredients:

- Four chicken breasts (about 1½ lb.)
- 3 tbsp. basil pesto
- 8 oz. mozzarella
- ½ tsp. salt
- ¼ tsp. black pepper

Directions:

1. Preheat oven to 350 F.
2. Coat heating dish with cooking spray. Put the chicken in the base in a single layer and sprinkle with the salt and pepper.
3. Spread the pesto on the bird. Put the mozzarella on top.
4. Heat for 35-45 minutes until the cheddar is bubbly.
5. Serve.

Nutrition: Calories 471 Fat 22 g Carbs 3.4 g Protein 61 g

SOUP AND STEWS

Best Broccoli Cheddar Soup

Ingredients

- 1 head fresh broccoli, chopped
- 1 (2 ounce) package dry cauliflower soup mix
- 4 cups water
- 1/2 cup milk
- 1 1/2 cups shredded Cheddar cheese

Directions:

1. Combine water and soup mix in a medium-sized stockpot over medium heat and stir often until well-blended.
2. Add the broccoli florets. Cover the pot partially and let it simmer for 5-10 minutes while stirring frequently.
3. Pour the soup in a blender or food processor once the broccoli is tender. Puree the soup. Pour the pureed soup back into the stockpot and stir in milk.
4. Add the cheese into the soup mixture and keep one half cup aside. Mix well until the cheese is melted. On top of each soup bowls, sprinkle them with the remaining 1/2 cup of cheese.

Nutrition: Calories: 262 calories; Total Carbohydrate: 14.9 Cholesterol: 47 Protein: 15.8 Total Fat: 16.2 Sodium: 923

Best Cream of Broccoli Soup

Preparation Time: 15 minutes

Cooking Time: 20 minutes

Servings: 3-4

Ingredients

- 2 tablespoons butter
- 1 onion, chopped
- 1 stalk celery, chopped
- 3 cups chicken broth
- 8 cups broccoli florets
- 3 tablespoons butter
- 3 tablespoons all-purpose flour
- 2 cups milk
- ground black pepper to taste

Directions:

1. In a medium-sized stockpot, heat 2 tablespoons of butter, and sauté celery and onion until soft. Add broth and broccoli; put a cover on and simmer, about 10 minutes.
2. In a blender, add the soup just enough to fill the pitcher halfway full. Keep the lids of the blender securely using a folded kitchen towel. Cautiously turn on the blender, get the soup moving with several quick pulses and then let it on to puree. Puree by batches until smooth and put into a

clean pot. Or you can puree the soup right in the cooking pot using a stick blender.

3. Heat 3 tablespoons butter in a small saucepan over medium heat; mix in flour and pour in the milk. Whisk until bubbly and thick, and add to soup. Use pepper to season and enjoy.

Nutrition: Calories: 207 calories; Sodium: 528 Total Carbohydrate: 17 Cholesterol: 32 Protein: 9.2 Total Fat: 12.4

Curried Butternut Squash Soup

Preparation Time: 10 minutes

Cooking Time: 45 minutes

Servings: 4

Ingredients:

- 2 tablespoons olive oil, divided
- 6 cups chopped butternut squash
- 1 large sweet onion, chopped
- 1 tablespoon fresh grated ginger
- 1 tablespoon minced garlic
- 2 teaspoons curry powder
- ¼ teaspoon ground mustard powder
- Salt and pepper to taste
- 4 cups chicken stock (low sodium)

Directions:

1. Heat 1 tablespoon oil in a large saucepan over medium heat. Add the butternut squash and sauté for 6 to 8 minutes until browned. Spoon the squash into a bowl and reheat the skillet with the remaining oil.
2. Add the onions, curry powder, garlic, ginger, mustard powder, salt and pepper. Cook for 4 to 6 minutes until the onions are translucent. Add the squash back to the pot along with the chicken stock.

3. Bring to a boil then reduce heat and simmer, covered, for 45 minutes. Turn off the heat and puree the soup using an immersion blender until smooth. Spoon into bowls and serve hot.

Nutrition: 275 Calories 32g Carbs 13g Fat 7g Protein

Roasted Tomato Basil Soup

Preparation Time: 15 minutes

Cooking Time: 30 minutes

Servings: 4

Ingredients:

- 4 large vine-ripened tomatoes, sliced
- 1 large sweet onion, sliced
- 6 cloves fresh garlic, sliced
- Olive oil, as needed
- Salt and pepper
- 2 cups vegetable broth
- 2 tablespoons tomato paste
- ¼ cup fresh chopped basil

Directions:

1. Preheat the oven to 350°F. Spread the tomatoes, onions, and garlic on a foil-lined baking sheet and drizzle with oil. Season with salt and pepper then toss gently.
2. Roast for 40 minutes, stirring once halfway through, until very tender. Heat the vegetable stock in a large saucepan over medium heat. Whisk in the tomato paste and basil then add the roasted vegetables. Bring to a boil then reduce heat and simmer, covered, for 10 minutes.

3. Turn off the heat and puree the soup using an immersion blender until smooth. Spoon into bowls and serve hot.

Nutrition: 90 Calories 18g Carbs 5g Fat 4g Protein

Creamy Sweet Potato Soup

Preparation Time: 15 minutes

Cooking Time: 35 minutes

Servings: 4

Ingredients:

- 1 tablespoon coconut oil
- 2 medium sweet onions, chopped
- 3 cloves minced garlic
- 6 cups chopped sweet potatoes
- 4 cups chicken broth (low sodium)
- ½ teaspoon ground cinnamon
- Salt and pepper

Directions:

1. Heat the coconut oil in a large saucepan over medium-high heat. Stir in the onions and garlic then cook for 5 to 6 minutes until tender. Add the sweet potatoes and sauté for 5 minutes.
2. Stir in the broth then bring to a boil. Reduce heat and simmer, covered, for 20 minutes until the vegetables are tender. Turn off the heat and puree the soup using an immersion blender until smooth. Season with cinnamon, salt and pepper and serve hot.

Nutrition: 110 Calories 23g Carbs 1g Fat 2g Protein

Hearty Beef and Vegetable Stew

Preparation Time: 10 minutes

Cooking Time: 30 minutes

Servings: 1

Ingredients:

- 1 tablespoon olive oil
- 2 medium sweet potatoes, peeled and chopped
- 2 large carrots, peeled and sliced
- 1 large yellow onion, chopped
- 1 cup sliced celery
- 1-pound beef stew meat, chopped
- 2 (14-ounce) cans diced tomatoes
- 4 cups beef stock (low sodium)
- 1 teaspoon fresh chopped rosemary
- ½ teaspoon fresh chopped thyme
- Salt and pepper

Directions:

1. Heat the oil in a large saucepan over medium-high heat. Add the sweet potatoes, carrots, onion, and celery and cook for 4 to 5 minutes until lightly browned. Stir in the beef along with the tomatoes, stock, and seasonings.
2. Bring the mixture to a boil then reduce heat and simmer, covered, for one hour – stir every 15

minutes. Uncover the pot and simmer for another 45 minutes then serve hot.

Nutrition: 385 Calories 21g Carbs 19g Fat 44g Protein

VEGETABLES

Innovated Shrimp Salad

Preparation Time: 10 minutes

Cooking Time: 10 minutes

Servings: 2

Ingredients:

- tablespoons coarsely chopped mint
- teaspoon curry powder
- Kirby cucumbers
- 16 large shrimp
- 1/4 cup plus 1 tablespoon extra-virgin olive oil
- Salt and freshly ground black pepper
- 1 tablespoon fresh lime juice
- Sugar, for sprinkling
- packed cups mâché
- 1 pound red and yellow watermelons
- 1/4 cup salted roasted pistachios
- 1/2 cup Greek-style whole-milk yogurt

Directions:

1 Shell and devein the shrimp Use a medium bowl and mix the 1 tablespoon of olive oil with the curry powder then pour in the shrimp and toss to

coat well. Cover the bowl with the shrimp mix with plastic wrap and place in the fridge for 1 hour. Wash and dry the cucumbers and cut them into thin spears place them in another medium bowl and combine them with the lime juice and mint; toss and season as desired with salt and pepper. Also cover with plastic wrap and place in the fridge. Cut the watermelon into flat triangles lay them flat on a tray and sprinkle them with sugar (on one side only) Take a grill pan and heat it over medium high heat. Grill the watermelon with the sugared side until charred not burnt. Place a skillet over medium heat and add 2 tablespoons of olive oil pour in the shrimp and season it with salt and pepper. Cook the shrimp for around 1 to 2 minutes on each side until it is white throughout. Take the bowl with the cucumber mix and add in the remaining 2 tablespoons of olive oil and the mâché season with salt and pepper; toss. Use a small bowl and mix the yogurt with salt as desired then take 4 small salad plates and dollop the yogurt on each plate top with the grilled watermelon and then the shrimp. Use a spoon to retrieve all the curry oil left in the skillet and drizzle it over the shrimp Place a portion of the cucumber mix on each plate and top with pistachios; serve immediately.

Nutrition: 120 calories 3g fiber 10g fats

Citrusy Scallops with Pomegranate

Preparation Time: 15 minutes

Cooking Time: 5 minutes

Servings: 2

Ingredients:

- 1 ruby red grapefruit
- clementine
- Crushed red pepper
- Salt
- Extra-virgin olive oil
- 8 large dry diver sea scallops
- cups baby arugula
- 1/2 cup pomegranate seeds
- 1/2 small red onion, finely julienned 2 cloves garlic, smashed

Directions:

1 Peel the red grapefruit and cut it into segments put in a medium sized bowl 2. Peel the 3 clementine and cut them into segments and pour them in the grapefruit. Sprinkle a pinch of salt over the grapefruit and also a dash of crushed red pepper mix to combine and set aside. Heat a large sauté pan with olive oil, when it is hot and but not smoking or burning add in the smashed garlic cloves. When the garlic has turned golden

in color remove from the heat and spoon out the garlic and discard it. Take the scallops and season them with salt, place the pan back on the heat and carefully lay the scallops in it. Cook each side until nicely caramelized (around 2 to 3 minutes per side make sure the heat is low to not smoke or burn the scallops). Remove from pan when the ready. Take a small bowl and put the arugula in it then pour over some of the juice from the bowl with the grapefruit and clementine, drizzle with extra-virgin olive oil and salt as desired. Toss to coat well. Add in half of the grapefruit and Clementine, the onion and another sprinkle of olive oil. Toss again. (The other half of the grapefruit and clementine can be stored for other use or discarded). Cut the scallops in halves. Place the arugula mix on 4 nice salad dishes then place the cut scallops over the arugula and top with sprinkled pomegranate seeds.

Nutrition: 113 calories 2g fiber 11g fats

Brisk Mediterranean Chicken Salad

Preparation Time: 10 minutes

Cooking Time: 10 minutes

Serving: 2

Ingredients:

- teaspoons tarragon vinegar
- tablespoons olive oil
- 1/2 tablespoon fresh lemon juice
- 1 tablespoon chopped fresh tarragon
- 1/2 tablespoon Dijon mustard
- 1 1/2 tablespoons drained capers
- 1/3 cup dried currants
- 1/2 cup coarsely chopped pitted Kalamata olives
- 1 cup halved cherry tomatoes
- 1/2 cup orzo
- 1 6-ounce jar marinated artichoke heart
- cups diced cooked chicken

Directions:

1 Whisk the vinegar, oil, lemon juice, tarragon and mustard in a small bowl, blend well and then season with salt and pepper. Use a medium size bowl and place the chicken in it with ¼ cup of dressing. Place a large pot of salted water to boil and then cook the orzo until it is firm to bite but tender and then drain. Rinse the orzo under cold

water and then drain well. Place the orzo in a large bowl and mix in the remaining dressing. Add in the, tomatoes, capers, currants, olives, artichoke hearts and chicken. Toss everything around to coat well. Season with a little more salt and pepper and serve.

Nutrition: 123 calories 7g fats 2g fiber

Spicy Tamarind Tinged Shrimp Salad

Preparation Time: 10 minutes

Cooking Time: 15 minutes

Servings: 2

Ingredients:

- For the dressing:
- Salt, to taste
- tablespoons fresh lime juice
- tablespoons soy sauce
- tablespoons Asian sesame oil
- Ashes dashes Asian hot chili oil
- For the shrimp mix:
- pounds large shrimp
- 1 small onion
- 1 cup loosely packed mint leaves
- 1 teaspoon tamarind paste
- 1 tablespoon minced gingerroot
- 1/3 cup water
- 12 black peppercorns
- 1 teaspoon ground cumin
- 1/2 teaspoon sugar
- Salt, to taste
- Vegetable oil spray
- For the vegetables:
- cup loosely packed cilantro leaves

- cups diced celery
- scallions, minced
- cups shredded iceberg lettuce
- cups shredded red cabbage
- cups grated carrots
- tablespoons toasted sesame seeds, for garnish

Directions:

1 Start by making the shrimp mix. Take a food processor (or blender) and combine the onion, mint leaves, tamarind paste, minced gingerroot, 1/3 cup water, black peppercorns (coarsely crushed), ground cumin, sugar and salt. Puree and transfer the mix to a bow add in the shrimp, toss to coat and set it aside to marinate, while you go preparing the salad and dressing mix. Take a bowl and whisk jointly the 6 ingredients for the salad dressing, make sure everything combines well. Make sure all the vegetables for the salad have been properly washed, dried and cut or shredded as indicated then mix them all in a salad bowl. Place a large skillet over high heat and spray it with the vegetable oil, when it is hot stir in the shrimp and cook it for around 3 to 4 minutes turning them over every so often to prevent burning them. Once cooked remove from heat chill for a bit about 1 to 2 minutes. Add the shrimp to the vegetable mix pour over the salad dressing and toss to coat. Sprinkle the toasted

sesame over the shrimp salad to garnish and serve.

Nutrition: 116 calories 20g fats 6g fiber

Natural Lobster Salad

Preparation Time: 10 minutes

Cooking Time: 15 minutes

Servings: 2

Ingredients:

- 1 1/2-pound lobsters
- Salt
- 1/2 cup peas
- 1/2 tablespoons fresh lemon juice
- 1/4 cup extra-virgin olive oil
- 1 tablespoon coarsely chopped basil
- 1/2 cup thinly sliced celery
- Freshly ground white pepper
- 1 teaspoon finely grated lemon zest
- 1 small lettuce

Directions:

1 Put a large pot of salted water to boil. When it is boiling carefully add in the lobsters. Cover the pot, turn the heat to high and cook for about 7 to 9 minutes until the lobsters are bright red. Remove the lobsters from the pot by using tongs, transfer them to a bowl set aside and allow them to chill. Once the lobsters are cool enough to handle, remove the meat from the lobsters by cracking the knuckles and claws. (If the claws

have rubber bands remove bands first) Use a scissors to slit open the shells of the tail to remove the meat from there as well. Make sure you get rid of the dark intestinal veins from the lobsters 'tails. Now slice the lobster meat into pieces about ½ of an inch thick. Use a small saucepan and boil some water to cook the peas. Cook them for about 2 minutes until they are tender then drain them well. Thinly slice the shallot and set aside Use a large bowl to mix the lemon juice, olive oil, celery, sliced shallot and lemon zest once mixed add in the peas and lobster season with the white pepper and salt; toss to combine everything well. Wash drain and shred the lettuce on to a nice serving platter and then pour the lobster mix over the bed of lettuce and serve.

Nutrition: 113 calories 5g fiber 12g carbs

SNACK AND DESSERTS

Chocolate Cupcakes

Preparation Time: 5 Minutes

Cooking Time: 20 Minutes

Servings: 6

Ingredients:

- 1 ½ cups of almond flour
- 1 cup shredded coconut
- Two large eggs
- ¼ cup cream cheese
- 3 tbsp plain Greek yogurt
- ¼ cup swerve
- 2 tbsp cocoa powder, unsweetened
- 3 tbsp butter
- 2 tsp baking powder
- Spices:
- 1 tsp vanilla extract

Directions:

1. In a large mixing bowl, place eggs and butter. Beat well on high speed until light and fluffy mixture. Then add swerve, cream cheese, and Greek yogurt. Continue to mix until smooth.

2. Finally, add almond flour, shredded coconut, and baking powder. Mix well.
3. Divide the mixture between 6 silicone cups and set aside.
4. Plugin the instant pot and position a trivet at the bottom of the inner pot. Pour in 1 cup of water and carefully place cups on the trivet.
5. Put the timer for 10 minutes on the ''Manual'' mode.
6. Perform a rapid pressure release and open the lid. Remove the cups from the pot and cool to room temperature.

Nutrition: Calories 212 Total Fats: 18.9g Carbs: 4.2g Protein: 6g

Chocolate Chip Mug Cake

Preparation Time: 5 Minutes

Cooking Time: 10 Minutes

Servings: 1

Ingredients:

- 3 tbsp almond flour
- 3 tbsp coconut oil, softened
- 1 tbsp cocoa powder, unsweetened
- 1 tbsp chocolate chips, unsweetened
- ½ tsp baking powder
- 2 tsp swerve

Spices:

- ¼ tsp vanilla extract

Directions:

1. In a small bowl, combine the ingredients and mix well until fully incorporated. Transfer the mixture to an oven-safe mug and loosely cover with aluminum foil.
2. Plugin the instant pot, then pour in one cup of water.
3. Place a trivet at the bottom of the inner pot and place the mug on top.
4. Press the "Manual" button and set the timer for 5 minutes on high pressure.

5. When done, perform a quick pressure release and open the lid. Cool for a while and serve.

Nutrition: Calories 464 Total Fats: 48g Carbs: 9.1g Protein: 3.3g

Treats & Trinkets

Creamy Coconut Hazelnut Cake

Preparation Time: 5 Minutes

Cooking Time: 35 Minutes

Servings: 10

Ingredients:

- 2 cups coconut flour
- ¼ cup almond flour
- 3 tbsp shredded coconut
- 3 tsp baking powder
- 1 cup coconut cream
- Five large eggs
- ¼ cup erythritol
- 2 cups whipping cream, sugar-free
- 3 tbsp hazelnuts, finely chopped

Spices:

- 2 tsp vanilla extract

Directions:

1. Plugin the instant pot and pour in one cup of water. Place a trivet at the bottom of the inner pot, then set aside,
2. In a large mixing bowl, combine all dry fixings and mix well.
3. Put eggs, one at a time, then beat well on medium-high speed.

4. Now add coconut cream and vanilla extract. Continue to beat for two more minutes on medium speediness
5. Grease a small pan with some coconut oil and pour in the mixture.
6. In the pot, place the mixture and seal the lid.
7. Next, you need to set the steam release handle, then press the ''Manual'' button.
8. Set the timer for 20 minutes on high pressure.
9. Beat the whipping cream and wait until light and fluffy.
10. Add chopped hazelnuts and optionally some finely chopped almonds.
11. Refrigerate until use.
12. When you hear the cooker's end signal, perform a quick pressure release, and open the lid. Remove the pan from the pot and cool for a while.
13. Top with whipped cream and refrigerate for 2-3 hours before serving.

Nutrition: Calories 217 Total Fats: 18.2g Carbs: 5.1g Protein: 5.8g

Ice Cream Brownies

Preparation Time: 5 Minutes

Cooking Time: 40 Minutes

Servings: 6

Ingredients:

For the brownies:

- 1 cup almond flour
- ¼ cup coconut flour
- ¼ cup shredded coconut
- 1 tsp baking powder
- Three large eggs
- ¼ cup butter, melted
- 3 tbsp granulated stevia

For the ice cream:

- 1 cup plain Greek yogurt
- ¼ cup whipping cream
- ½ tsp agar powder
- 1 tbsp lemon zest
- 2 tsp vanilla extract
- ¼ cup swerve

Directions:

1. In a large mixing bowl, put Greek yogurt, whipping cream, agar powder, lemon zest, vanilla extract, and swerve. With a paddle attachment

on, beat well on medium-high speed until light and fluffy. Transfer to the refrigerator and set aside.

2. Now, prepare the brownies. Combine all dry ingredients and mix well. Put eggs, one at a time, then beat well with a paddle attachment on. Pour in the melted butter and continue to beat until fully incorporated.
3. Line a small cake pans with some parchment paper and adds the brownie mixture. Using a kitchen spatula, flatten the surface as evenly as possible and tightly wrap with aluminum foil.
4. Plugin the instant pot and pour in 1 cup of water. Set the trivet and add the cake pan.
5. Cook for 15 minutes on high pressure.
6. When done, perform a quick pressure release and open the lid.
7. Cautiously remove the pan from the pot and cool it to room temperature.
8. Top with the ice cream mixture and refrigerate for about an hour.

Nutrition: Calories 174 Total Fats: 14.2g Net Carbs: 3.3g Protein: 5.3g

Mint Brownies with Hazelnuts

Preparation Time: 5 Minutes

Cooking Time: 35 Minutes

Servings: 6

Ingredients:

- ¾ cup almond flour
- ½ cup flaxseed meal
- ½ cup Mascarpone
- Four large eggs
- 2 tbsp butter
- ¼ cup swerve
- 3 tbsp hazelnuts, finely chopped
- Spices:
- ¼ tsp salt
- 1 tsp mint extract

Directions:

1. Combine the fixings in a large mixing bowl and beat well on medium speed until fully incorporated and smooth.
2. Line a small cake pans with parchment paper and brush with some oil. Pour in the batter and loosely cover with aluminum foil.
3. Plugin the instant pot and set the trivet in the inner pot. Pour in approximately one cup of water and place the cake pan on top.

4. Seal the lid and set the steam release grip to the "Sealing" position. Press the "Manual" button and set the timer for 25 minutes.
5. When completed, perform a rapid pressure release and open the lid. Prudently remove the pan from the pot and chill for a while.
6. Slice into eight brownies and serve.

Nutrition: Calories 203 Total Fats: 15.8g Net Carbs: 1.6gProtein: 9.4g

Mocha Pots de Creme

Preparation Time: 5 Minutes

Cooking Time: 25 Minutes

Servings: 4

Ingredients:

- Two large eggs, separated
- 1 cup milk, full-fat
- ¾ cup heavy cream
- 3 tbsp stevia powder
- 2 tbsp cocoa powder, unsweetened
- 3 tbsp brewed espresso

Spices:

- ¼ tsp salt
- 1 tsp vanilla extract

Directions:

1. Put eggs, cocoa powder, espresso, stevia powder, vanilla, and salt. Set aside.
2. Plugin the instant pot and press the "Sauté" button. Pour in the milk and heavy cream. Give it a good stir and warm up.
3. Press the "Cancel" button, then gradually pour the warm milk mixture over the egg mixture, whisking constantly.

4. Divide the mixture between 4 ramekins and loosely cover with aluminum foil.
5. Arrange a trivet at the bottom of your pot and pour in 2 cups of water. Gently place the ramekins on top and seal the lid.
6. Put the steam release handle to the "Sealing" position and press the "Manual" button.
7. Cook for 15 minutes.
8. When done, perform a quick pressure release and open the lid. Remove the ramekins and transfer them to a wire rack. Cool to room temperature and then refrigerate for about an hour.

Nutrition: Calories 257 Total Fats: 25.5g Net Carbs: 3.5g Protein: 5.5g

Chocolate Chip Pudding

Preparation Time: 5 Minutes

Cooking Time: 15 Minutes

Servings: 4

Ingredients:

- 1 cup unsweetened almond milk
- ¼ cup swerve
- 1 tbsp agar powder
- ¼ cup almonds, finely chopped
- 2 tbsp cocoa powder, unsweetened
- 2 tbsp chocolate chips, sugar-free
- One ¼ cup whipping cream
- ½ cup coconut cream
- Spices:
- 1 tsp vanilla extract

Directions:

1. Plugin the instant pot and pour in the milk. Press the ''Sauté'' button and heat up. Add swerve, cocoa powder, coconut cream, and vanilla extract.
2. Bring it to a boil, stirring constantly, and then add agar powder. Continue to cook for 1-2 minutes.
3. Press the ''Cancel'' button and stir in finely chopped almonds.

4. Transfer the combination to a large mixing bowl and pour in the whipping cream. Beat well at high speed for 2-3 minutes.
5. Finally, divide the mixture between serving bowls and cool completely before serving.

Nutrition: Calories 257Total Fats: 24.5g Net Carbs: 6.5g Protein: 3.9g

Vanilla Cherry Panna Cotta

Preparation Time: 5 Minutes

Cooking Time: 15 Minutes

Servings: 2

Ingredients:

For the vanilla layer:

- 1 cup heavy whipping cream
- 2 tbsp whole milk
- 1 tsp agar powder
- ½ tsp vanilla extract
- 1 tbsp walnuts, roughly chopped

For the cherry layer:

- 1 cup heavy whipping cream
- 1 tsp agar powder
- 1 tbsp almonds, roughly chopped
- 2 tsp cherry extract

Directions:

1. Plugin the instant pot and combine all vanilla layer ingredients in the stainless-steel insert. Press the "Sauté" button and stir constantly. Let it simmer and then press the "Cancel" button. Transfer to a large bowl and set aside.
2. Clean the pot and pat dry with kitchen paper.

3. Add all cherry layer ingredients and stir well. Again, bring it to a light simmer, stirring constantly.
4. Pour about the ½-inch thick vanilla layer in a medium-sized glass.
5. Now, pour the second layer of the cherry combination. Do the process again until you have used both mixtures.
6. Garnish with some fresh mint and refrigerate for at least 1 hour before serving.
7. Enjoy!

Nutrition: Calories 467 Total Fats: 48.7g Net Carbs: 4.6g Protein: 4.5g

Orange Lime Pudding

Preparation Time: 5 Minutes

Cooking Time: 10 Minutes

Servings: 4

Ingredients:

- ¼ cup almond milk, unsweetened
- 1 tsp agar powder
- ¼ cup coconut cream
- ¼ cup whipping cream
- 1 tbsp stevia powder
- 1 tbsp coconut oil

Spices:

- 1 tsp orange extract
- 1 tsp lime zest, freshly grated

Directions:

1. Plugin your instant pot and place coconut oil in the stainless-steel insert. Press the "Sauté" button and gently stir with a wooden spatula.
2. When melted, add almond milk, coconut cream, and whipping cream. Bring it to a light simmer, stirring continually.
3. Stir in the stevia powder, agar powder, and orange extract. Cook for another 2-3 minutes, stirring constantly.

4. Turn off the pot and pour the pudding into serving bowls or ramekins immediately.
5. Let it cool to room temperature. Sprinkle with lime zest and refrigerate for 1 hour before serving.
6. Enjoy!

Nutrition: Calories 155 Total Fats: 12.3g Net Carbs: 10.7 Protein: 0.7g

Guacamole Deviled Eggs

Preparation Time: 15 Minutes

Cooking Time: 0 Minutes

Servings: 4

Ingredients:

- Eight large eggs
- ½ cup chopped avocado
- Two tablespoons canned coconut milk
- One tablespoon chopped cilantro
- One teaspoon fresh lime juice
- ¼ teaspoon ground cumin
- Salt and pepper to taste
- Paprika for garnish

Directions:

1. Put the eggs in a pan, then cover with water.
2. Bring the water to a boil, then remove from heat and let rest for 10 minutes.
3. Rinse the eggs in cold water until cool enough to handle, then peel.
4. Cut the eggs in half and spoon the yolks into a bowl.
5. Add the avocado, coconut milk, cilantro, lime juice, and cumin.
6. Season with pepper and salt, then stir until smooth.

7. Spoon or pipe the mixture into the egg halves, then sprinkle with paprika.

Nutrition: Calories 185 Fat 15g Protein 12g Net Carbs 2g

Double Chocolate Chip Cookies

Preparation Time: 15 minutes plus 2 hours chilling time

Cooking Time: 10 to 12 minutes

Servings: 6

Ingredients:

- ½ cup plus 2 tablespoons all-purpose flour
- ⅓ cup unsweetened natural cocoa powder
- ¼ teaspoon baking soda
- ⅛ teaspoon salt
- tablespoons unsalted butter, at room temperature
- tablespoons packed brown sugar
- tablespoons granulated sugar
- 1 large egg white
- ½ teaspoon vanilla extract
- ½ cup semisweet chocolate chips

Directions:

1 In a small bowl, whisk the flour, cocoa powder, baking soda, and salt.

2 In a medium bowl, cream together the butter, brown sugar, and granulated sugar for about 1 minute until light and fluffy.

3 One at a time, add the egg white and vanilla, whisking well after each addition until combined.

4. Stir in the flour mixture just until combined and fold in the chocolate chips. Cover tightly with plastic wrap and refrigerate for at least 2 hours, or up to 24.
5. Preheat the oven to 350°F.
6. Line a baking sheet with a silicone mat (or parchment paper).
7. Divide the dough into 6 equal balls and place them on the prepared sheet at least 2 inches apart. Flatten them slightly with the palm of your hand and bake for 10 to 12 minutes until the cookies look set. Cool the cookies on the baking sheet for at least 10 minutes before devouring.

Nutrition: 165 calories 7.1g carbs 6.3g protein

CPSIA information can be obtained
at www.ICGtesting.com
Printed in the USA
BVHW092050190421
605311BV00002B/130

9 781802 330380